WILLIE LYNCHISM

THE Secret History Lesson:
A Personal Discovery of TRUE American History

Compiled and Written by

Karla "With a K" Edward

authorHOUSE®

AuthorHouse™ LLC
1663 Liberty Drive
Bloomington, IN 47403
www.authorhouse.com
Phone: 1-800-839-8640

Published by AuthorHouse 1/16/2014

ISBN: 978-1-4918-4733-6 (sc)
ISBN: 978-1-4918-4732-9 (e)

Library of Congress Control Number: 2013923302

Any people depicted in stock imagery provided by Thinkstock are models,
and such images are being used for illustrative purposes only.
Certain stock imagery © Thinkstock.

This book is printed on acid-free paper.

CONTENTS

FOREWORD

"History," according to Mandell Creighton, "provides no compensation for suffering, nor penalties for wrong. In order to fully understand history, one must vow to accept the truth, regardless of how painful said truths might be."

For two hundred and forty eight years, Africans in America (slaves), were governed according to a fixed set of rules that transformed them into seeing themselves as Niggers, then Coloreds, Blacks, Negroes, African Americans and for some, ultimately back to Niggers/Niggas, again.

In spite of the passage of time, many things remain the same: we still control less than 1% of the wealth in this country, we still have the highest number of incarcerations, we're still marching and calling for justice and we do not have a complete understanding of history.

African American consciousness was captured and forcibly locked into Europe's racist pathological system, where it was forged into a character that is lacking for many.

Upon further review of this character, one readily sees the aim of those who shaped it, directly and indirectly. While it can be argued that the previous statement is a scathing opportunity to bait the races and rant, African Americans are, nevertheless, vexed over the discontinuity and inexplicable toxic miasma that's suffocating Black people.

Needless to say, the point that must be taken from my description of African American history, pre and post slavery, as it relates to the Willie Lynch Letter/Plan's inconspicuous trusteeship between the rulers of this land and their subjects, can be attributed to African Americans' powerlessness.

This scholarly feature challenges the supposition that the United States History Content Standards omit factual, historical events, which inspired the author to advocate for the entry of this painful, yet true history lesson, "Willie Lynchishm," in schools across America.

As a former educator in the Los Angeles Unified School District's public school system, Edward has witnessed countless numbers of minority students grappling with historical content that honors iconoclastic slave owners, among them, five of our first seven presidents: George Washington, Thomas Jefferson, James Madison, James Monroe, Andrew Jackson and Martin Van Buren.

Though scholar's descriptions of social and economic "constants" glorify capitalism, the despicable Eurocentric concepts of chattel slavery and colonialism are the cornerstones of Western Civilization. While the design of Chattel Slavery, The Willie Lynch Letter/Plan and Eugenics may very well be beyond belief, said provisions will never gain acceptance as long as they reside in a vacuum, which is also part of the plan.

Edward alarms us by removing the "plan" from that vacuum by writing this book.

Now, that action has taken place to fortify the phenomenon: establishing Dr. King's birthday as a national holiday and electing a Black President, it is politically correct to address the "what" aspect of the Willie Lynch Plan.

Yes, there was/is a grand design in place to ensure that Western thought shapes the behavior and consciousness of Africans here and abroad. However, Africans don't readily discuss the "how/why" aspect of the plan, for, the "how/why" aspects of any problem, are fettered to power.

Edward's treatment identifies the effect the Willie Lynch Letter/Plan has had and is having on Americans today. She reminds us that we aren't really free, just conformed, lest we open the mind's eye to the truth.

Richard McGee, Master of Social Work/ACSW
University of Southern California, Los Angeles, CA

THE Secret History Lesson

In 1998, I discovered a lesson about the history of this country that I was never taught in school. It opened my eyes to the origin of the pain and devastation of a people who have been manipulated, bamboozled, deceived, denigrated, disparaged, maligned and premeditatedly victimized for centuries in America for the sake of money, property, greed and fear.

I finally understood the angst and cognitive dissonance I'd felt for many years as a Black woman in America, especially the discomfort I felt living in the cradle of Civil War America, Petersburg, VA.

Upon discovering the Willie Lynch Lesson in 1998 on the Internet, I had newfound compassion for the Black Man. I understood White people better and myself even more.

This Secret History Lesson shed light on the origin and perpetuation of the racial problems we face in America. It also explained the blind ignorance of prominent White, media pundits, like Sean Hanity, Bill O'Riley, Ann Coulter, Laura Ingraham and Rush Limbaugh, who, by the way, are younger than me or very close to my age. Hence, theoretically, they had a similar education in history, as I did, at the time we attended K-12.

The most disturbing part of my discovery was the revelation that Americans, including myself, had been so convincingly and successfully programmed through education, to believe lies we were taught, probably by commission, in some cases, rather than omission, by teachers we respected and admired. Surely, *they* couldn't have known this Secret Lesson and not taught it.

At any rate, many students had turned the hate generated by the lies we were taught, into a personal truth that took on all kinds of manifestations in later life.

I call the Willie Lynch Lesson "secret" because secrecy is the act of keeping things hidden, often out of fear and shame of someone finding out. Secrets usually consist of information that potentially has a negative impact on someone else--emotionally, physically, or financially.

Certainly, the keepers of the Willie Lynch Plan believed that if the secret were revealed, either accidentally or on purpose, the revelation could, in some way, cause harm to them and to those around them.

A secret contains an element of shame that privacy does not. According to www.Jung-At-Heart.com, "...we may keep something private for all kinds of reasons, but most of the time, we keep something secret out of fear and shame of what others would think if they knew. We keep something secret because we believe the cost of telling is so high that it's virtually not a choice at all. Privacy is voluntary; secrecy is not."

Willie Lynchism was truly a *secret* plan, belonging to a group of people who desired to create a "social being called the Negro" in America. Thanks to the Internet, it is no longer secret.

For many, the hate and psychic destruction cultivated by Willie Lynchism continues to affect people in the 21st century.

In Black people, we see evidence of self-hate, fear and self-degradation engendered by Willie Lynchism, through abortion, broken families, divorce, low rates of marriage, domestic violence and abuse, the pre-dominance of Blacks in prison, fatherless children, substance abuse, negative attitudes toward education and personal achievement.

In White people, we see evidence of the arrogance, denial, fear and guilt engendered by Willie Lynchism through high rates of domestic violence/abuse, substance abuse, adultery, molestation, DUIs, murder, hate crimes, discrimination, legal inequities, racial profiling, segregation, excessive greed, war, fear mongering and the unfathomable lack of respect by Tea Party Republicans for our first Black president, Barack Obama.

Update September 2013:
Our nation just celebrated the 50th Anniversary of the 1963 March on Washington, yet the subject of this book and this not-so-secret-anymore history of our country is still unknown to many adults, as well as current students in grades K-12.

By the remarks and presence of celebrities, politicians and civil rights activists who attended the Anniversary of the March, it is clear that understanding the significance of the original March is still important. There continues to be a need to acknowledge, educate and celebrate civil rights, not stop.

As I watched the speeches, acknowledgements, and tributes, I decided to FINALLY publish this book that I started at the turn of the 21st century. I see now, more than ever, that there is an even greater need to get this lesson included in United States History Content Standards for Grades 5-12.

MY-STORY

As a woman born over fifty years ago, in the midst of the Civil Rights Movement, when my mother attended rallies led by Martin Luther King, Jr., I never knew how the timing of my birth coincided with a critical juncture in the way students were educated in America. American History textbook authors had seriously altered the veracity of His-Story Education.

By the time I was ready to begin my education in 1964, true American history had already been tainted and significantly revised...to protect the guilty and confuse the innocent. Most *teachers* probably didn't even know the truth.

The authentic history of Americans, both Black and White, has been obscured beneath decades of mendacious textbooks, egregious educational policy, deceptive legislation, mis-educated teachers and complicit politicians.

Born in Monterey, CA, in 1958, I grew up as an "Army brat," the younger of two girls in a military family. My father was later stationed at Ft. Lee, VA, in the early 1960's. My mother, an educated, government employed, conscientious, Army wife and mother from Kansas City, MO, went to great lengths to shelter my sister and me from the racist practices inherent in Virginia's Prince George County pubic school system.

As an adult, I learned that she had attended a rally in Petersburg, where Dr. Martin Luther King spoke, encouraging people to peacefully resist bussing and racist practices wherever they found them.

My mother took heed and decided that if she couldn't successfully avoid having her kids bussed to racist, inadequate schools out in the Virginia boonies; she would use her next best weapon of influence—money---to send her kids where she chose---St. James Elementary School, a private, Catholic school in Hopewell, VA.

We lived in Ft. Lee's Jackson Circle, where my parents drove through a nearby "sundown town," Colonial Heights, almost daily.

I remained oblivious to the incessant racism that swirled around my innocent, eight-year-old head, as I played with my White and Black friends stationed on the base.

There seemed to be no difference in our homes, the food we ate, the activities we took part in, or the privileges we enjoyed on the base as we rode our bicycles, played "house" and swam in the military pools. We lived the epitome of "innocence is bliss."

WILLIE LYNCHISM: THE SECRET HISTORY LESSON, A PERSONAL DISCOVERY OF TRUE AMERICAN HISTORY
By Karla "With a K" Edward

I LEARNED I WAS BLACK

It wasn't until my father was stationed at Schofield Barracks, HI, that I realized I was Black and that being White might be worse than that-- in Hawaii. Hawaiian youth called the last day of school before summer recess, "Kill Haole Day" (pronounced, "howlie"). In Hawaiian language, "haole" originally meant foreign or foreigner, but over time, it simply meant "White people."

On the last day of school, young Hawaiian school kids would harass and beat up White kids, just for being White. I had never heard of such a thing.

I don't remember ever actually seeing a "beat down," but I certainly knew and never forgot about the custom I learned as a Black, 3rd and 4th grader living in Hawaii: Hawaiians don't like White people, but they aren't so crazy about Blacks either.

On "kill haole day," I was glad I was Black, however, because I didn't have to watch my back. But I still knew that the little Hawaiian girls didn't really like me. They just didn't have a day named in honor of kicking my butt.

Living in Hawaii was an eye opening experience where I finally learned, at the age of nine, that I was indeed a little Black girl and some people did not like me because of the color of my skin.

I felt isolated amidst the tough little Hawaiian girls at Our Lady of Sorrows Catholic School, but enjoyed learning Hawaiian customs that helped me bridge the gap between cultures. I cultivated friendships with Whites, Blacks, Asians and Hawaiians in my neighborhood of Wahiawa, HI.

WILLIE LYNCHISM: THE SECRET HISTORY LESSON, A PERSONAL DISCOVERY OF TRUE AMERICAN HISTORY
By Karla "With a K" Edward

BACK TO THE MAINLAND

Upon my father's retirement in 1968, we moved from Hawaii back to Petersburg, Virginia, a city rich in our country's Civil War history. It was also where my father had a career employment opportunity as he embarked on his new life and career after retiring from the Army.

He went to work at the Federal Reformatory (where former Washington, D. C. Mayor Marion Barry was incarcerated years later) as a Sports Supervisor, a position from which he retired; my mother, a career federal employee, ultimately retired from the Equal Employment Opportunity Office, at Ft. Lee, VA.

My mother enrolled my sister and me in Walnut Hill Elementary School in Petersburg, where I began the 4th grade. We moved into an all Black neighborhood off

Crater Road (site of the American Civil War's "Battle of the Crater") where I enjoyed sleepovers with my new "best friend," Debbie Taylor, a little White girl from my new school.

Our friendship was short lived, however, because we could not visit each other outside of school. Somehow, we drifted apart with no assistance from our parents to help keep our friendship alive. I didn't know why, so I just went with the flow, as kids do, and grew to appreciate my new neighborhood, as I made friends with kids who looked like me.

After about two years, we moved into the last house my father would ever live in, another all Black neighborhood, near Virginia State University--College Park, in Ettrick, VA.

I was enrolled in Mrs. Berry's 5th grade class at Ettrick Elementary, where I took my first stand against, what I perceived as racism from my teacher.

She insisted I call her "ma'am," and I refused. I am sure she saw me as an insolent, uppity, little Black bitch (now that I know how Virginia southerners her age really thought of us), more than a rebellious little Black girl she

WILLIE LYNCHISM: THE SECRET HISTORY LESSON, A PERSONAL DISCOVERY OF TRUE AMERICAN HISTORY
By Karla "With a K" Edward

wanted to suppress, because I made a huge deal out of this issue of her insisting I call her "ma'am."

Mrs. Berry took it up with my mother who assured me that as long as I did not disrespect my teacher, I did not have to call her, "ma'am. Calling her Mrs. Berry would do," a decision I was quire comfortable with.

I don't know how Mrs. Berry felt about it, because the rest of my time with her was very short, but I'm sure she got tired of hearing me say her name. I completed 5th and 6th grade, then went to private school in Petersburg for the 7th and 8th grade.

After experiencing the rituals and sacraments of Catholic school and seeing a young nun lose it in front of my 8th grade class and cursing us out, I asked my parents if I could attend the public school my neighbors attended, Matoaca High.

I would think that this public school in Chesterfield County, VA, even in 1972, would have teachers who knew the TRUE history of the region they lived in, but for the life of me, I just don't remember being taught that five of the first seven American presidents owned slaves. George

Washington being one of them. Nope, they skipped that part of the "founding fathers" lesson.

Perhaps they set that information aside, for me to learn later. Or could it be that they didn't know it themselves? After all, more than likely, they were also taught from the same misleading textbooks that sought to paint the U. S. in the most favorable light possible.

Or could it be that Mr. Fitzgerald, the thin, blonde, thirty something, History teacher, who faced our class of 10th graders, didn't quite know how to share some information about American Slavery with Black and White sixteen year olds, who were sowing their wild oats of rebellion anyway?

Whatever the case, if it is left up to the teachers who teach the textbook, students will never learn the truth about our "founding fathers," much less American Slavery. Even the young, very well trained, Teach For America teachers I later worked with in Los Angeles, would rather teach the Holocaust than American Slavery.

I went on to graduate from Matoaca High School in 1976, blissfully ignorant (education-wise) that American Slavery was actually a vicious hate crime that the American

 WILLIE LYNCHISM: THE SECRET HISTORY LESSON, A PERSONAL DISCOVERY OF TRUE AMERICAN HISTORY By Karla "With a K" Edward

education system was hiding. In my soul, however, I knew something about this subject was not fully divulged.

I wouldn't rest until I discovered the truth about American Slavery and the residual effects it has had on American society today for people of all races, creeds and colors. There *had* to be a reason we are so blissfully dysfunctional!

Fast forward twenty-two years when I had access to the Internet! It was 1997, when I discovered the Internet and I would unlock the door to TRUTH that I had never been taught in school.

I discovered Willie Lynch. Willie Lynchism. Willie Lynch Law. The origin of the term "lynch."

As I read the online document, *"Let's Make a Slave" by Willie Lynch* and *"The Origin and Development of a Social Being Called "The Negro,"* it became abundantly clear to me that American Slavery had, negatively affected Black people and White people alike. Just in different ways.

I also understood that Black and White Americans continue to be negatively affected by the lingering effects of this heinous social institution historians have sought desperately to obscure. Some History books have covered the subject in laughable ways, using the socially acceptable language of the day.

American Slavery, according to today's definition, would constitute a "hate crime" worthy of prosecution to the fullest extent of the law and its victims would certainly be due restitution or reparations.

Maybe I should call it "Restitution," just to give it a new name, since "Reparations" is so negatively charged. Nonetheless, to call it like it is, Reparations is an issue that remains unresolved for many in America's Black communities because the ugly truth is that the economic history of this country is based on American Slavery.

Whether we like it or not, this country was built on the backs of American Slaves who received no compensation. Now the keepers of THE Secret Lesson's biggest fear is that President Barack Obama will set up a system called ObamaCare, aka, The Affordable Care Act (ACA), to redistribute America's wealth by providing health care to all Americans. Not a chance. The ACA is not a free entitlement. It's simply a way for more Americans to afford to pay for healthcare that their job is not providing.

WILLIE LYNCHISM: THE SECRET HISTORY LESSON, A PERSONAL DISCOVERY OF TRUE AMERICAN HISTORY
By Karla "With a K" Edward

The step-by-step methods described in "Let's Make a Slave," outline the horrific processes executed by "planters" or slave owners to contain and restrain their chattel slaves by manipulation, through enslavement and/or mind control.

Some people argue that William "Willie" Lynch did not exist. They say he was not a real man. However, it is clear that whether William "Willie" Lynch was a real person or a fictitious name created for a story that outlined a process to destroy the authentic nature of African people, the plan to "create a social being called the Negro" was real and quite effective.

The petition is still online and your signature is welcome. Simply search the keyword phrase: *willie lynch online petition*

Have you ever heard of the Willie Lynch Speech of 1712?

- Yes, I've heard of it, but know nothing about it 41%
- Yes, I studied it in school 18%
- No 41%

poll data courtesy of www.karlawithak.net

WILLIE LYNCHISM: THE SECRET HISTORY LESSON,
A PERSONAL DISCOVERY OF TRUE AMERICAN HISTORY
By Karla "With a K" Edward

WILLIE LYNCH
SPEECH OF 1712

GIVEN ON THE BANKS OF THE
JAMES RIVER IN VIRGINIA

Gentlemen, I greet you here on the bank of the James River in the year of our Lord one Thousand seven hundred and twelve.

First, I shall thank you, the gentlemen of the Colony of Virginia, for bringing me here. I am here to help you solve some of your problems with slaves.

Your invitation reached me on my modest plantation in the West Indies where I have experimented with some of the newest and still the oldest methods for control of slaves.

Ancient Rome would envy us if my program was implemented. As our boat sailed south on the James River, named for our illustrious King, whose version of the Bible we cherish, I saw enough to know that your problem is not unique.

While Rome used cords of wood as crosses for standing human bodies along its old highways in great numbers, you are here using the tree and the rope on occasion. I caught the whiff of a dead slave hanging from a tree a couple of miles back.

You are not only losing valuable stock by hangings, you are having uprisings, slaves are running away, your crops are sometimes left in the fields too long for maximum profit, you suffer occasional fires, your animals are killed.

Gentlemen, you know what your problem[s] are; I do not need to elaborate; I am not here to enumerate your problems. I am here to introduce you to a method of solving them.

In my bag here, I have a foolproof method for controlling your Black slaves, I guarantee every

WILLIE LYNCHISM: THE SECRET HISTORY LESSON, A PERSONAL DISCOVERY OF TRUE AMERICAN HISTORY
By Karla "With a K" Edward

one of you, that if installed correctly it will control the slaves for at least three hundred years.

Note: In 2009, we were 297 years from 1712 and this "action plan" was still in effect for many Americans, in spite of the fact that we'd elected our first African American president.

My method is simple. Any member of your family or your overseer can use it.

I have outlined a number of differences among the slaves: and I take these differences and make them bigger.

I use fear and envy for control purposes.

These methods have worked on my modest plantation in the West Indies and it will work throughout the South. Take this simple little list of differences, and think about them.

On top of my list is "Age" but it is there only because it starts with an "A"; the second is "Color" or shade, there is intelligence, size, sex, size of plantations, status on plantation, attitude of owners, whether the slaves live in the valley, on the hill, East, West, North, South, have fine hair, coarse hair, or is tall or short.

Now that you have a list of differences, I shall give you an outline of action - but before that I shall assure you that distrust is stronger than trust, and envy is stronger than adulation, respect or admiration.

The Black slave, after receiving this indoctrination, shall carry on and will become self re-fueling and self-generating for hundreds of years, maybe thousands.

Don't forget you must pitch the old Black male vs. the young Black male, and the young Black male against the old Black male.

You must use the dark skin slave vs. the light skin slaves and the light skin slaves vs. the dark skin

WILLIE LYNCHISM: THE SECRET HISTORY LESSON,
A PERSONAL DISCOVERY OF TRUE AMERICAN HISTORY
By Karla "With a K" Edward

slaves. You must use the female vs. the male, and the male vs. the female.

You must also have your white servants and overseers distrust all Blacks, but it is necessary that your slaves trust and depend on us; they must love, respect and trust only us.

Gentlemen, these kits are your keys to control. Use them. Have your wives and children use them, never miss an opportunity. If used intensely for one year, the slaves themselves will remain perpetually distrustful. Thank you, gentlemen.

A white slave owner from the West Indies, William Lynch, delivered this speech to Virginia "planters" on the bank of the James River in 1712.

REVELATION OF THE PHENOMENON

Only after reading the scientific, methodical plan called, "Let's Make a Slave," will you truly understand why White historians and textbook publishers went to such lengths to keep American Slavery an abstruse topic in American history.

Now that we have the first African American President, Barack Obama, perhaps all Americans are ready to deal with the truth about this country's Founding Fathers, their ideology, lifestyle, behavior and hypocrisies.

The guarantee that the plan "will control the slaves for at least three hundred years" was well on course to the 300 year mark, until 2009, when 297 years later, several phenomena occurred.

WILLIE LYNCHISM: THE SECRET HISTORY LESSON,
A PERSONAL DISCOVERY OF TRUE AMERICAN HISTORY
By Karla "With a K" Edward

First, new technology, including the cell phone and the Internet became available to the consumer, then we saw the election and inauguration of America's first African American President, Barack Obama. President Obama used the power of the Internet to amass a tremendous following and win the 2008 Presidential election, which manifested the phenomena Willie Lynch spoke of, that could halt the course of this plan.

He prophetically stated, *"...unless a phenomenon occurs and re-shifts the positions of the male and female..."* the plan would be self-refueling.

President and First Lady Obama, along with their beautiful daughters, represent not only the quintessential Western family image for African Americans to adopt; they are worthy of emulation by any American family.

The "phenomenon" has occurred. Through our First Family we see the male and female roles re-shifted as the plan described. The madness can stop, after seeing the magnificent example of our 44th President's family and several other "phenomena" that have occurred if we just take the time to notice. However, the myths, lies and confusion persist because people still don't know the whole story.

American history textbook publishers have assiduously done the bidding of those who chose to revise the racist history of this nation.

As James W. Loewen argues in *"Lies My Teacher Told Me, Everything Your American History Textbook Got Wrong,"* that by glossing over America's racist past, history textbooks fall short of education's critical responsibility to explain the cause of racism, why it continues and how we might finally rid ourselves of its harmful legacy."

We need to ask ourselves as Americans, Black and White, why certain words elicit anger, angst and defensive postures. Why do right wing conservatives like Sean Hannity, Rush Limbaugh and Ann Coulter engender fear in their rhetoric and inject subtle hints of white supremacy, hoping to retain whatever advantages they feel they have and are desperate not to lose?

Their warnings of the return of the Fairness Doctrine are filled with misleading ambiguities and fear-mongering that relates to no one but a few of the right wing, talk-radio hosts that have been enriched by the divisive state of politics they created.

Their antics splintered our nation politically, bolstered George Bush's exit and served new-fangled radio hosts who found a creative way to work radio---by turning the best radio jobs into entrepreneurial franchises and commandeering the public airwaves to line their pockets.

Their strategy resembles that of major companies that took advantage of the opportunities to benefit financially from the American Slave trade---selfish greed, in the name of Capitalism, being the motivating factor.

AMERICAN COMPANIES THAT PROFITED FROM AMERICAN SLAVERY

According to Sidney Davis, a commenter on atlantablackstar.com, "American Slavery was the largest profit making enterprise the world has ever seen, bigger than Wall Street." He says that, "In fact, Wall Street was a Slave Market before it was a Financial Center."

Below are companies Davis found that reaped huge profits from the institution of American Slavery:

1. **Lehman Brothers**' business started with the slave trade. They recently admitted their role in the business of slavery. According to the Sun Times, the financial services firm acknowledged that its founding partners owned several slaves during the Civil War. It "profited

significantly" from American slavery. "This is a sad part of our heritage …We're deeply apologetic … It was a terrible thing … There's no one sitting in the United States in the year 2005, hopefully, who would ever, in a million years, defend the practice," said Joe Polizzotto, general counsel of Lehman Brothers.

2. **Aetna, Inc.,** the USA's largest health insurer, apologized for selling policies in the 1850s. The policies reimbursed slave owners financially when their slaves died. In 2002, Aetna spokesman Fred Laberge lamented, "We express our deep regret over any participation, at all, in this deplorable practice."

3. **JPMorgan Chase** recently admitted their company's links to slavery. "Today, we are reporting that this research found that, between 1831 and 1865, two of our predecessor banks—Citizens Bank and Canal Bank in Louisiana—accepted approximately 13,000 enslaved individuals as collateral on loans and took ownership of approximately 1,250 of them when the plantation owners defaulted on the loans," the company wrote in a statement.

4. **New York Life Insurance Company** is America's largest mutual life insurance company. Its growth is due to profits earned by selling insurance policies on slaves. According to USA Today, evidence of ten **New York Life** slave policies come from an 1847 account book kept by W.A. Britton, the company's Natchez, MS, agent. The book is part of a collection at Louisiana State University, which contains Britton's notes on slave policies he wrote for $375 to $600. According to New York Life history, 339 of the company's first 1,000 policies were written on the lives of slaves.

5. USA Today reported that **Wachovia Corporation** (now owned by Wells Fargo) has apologized for its ties to slavery, after disclosing that two of its predecessors owned slaves and accepted them as payment. "On behalf of Wachovia Corporation, I apologize to all Americans, and especially to African-Americans and people of African descent," said Ken Thompson, Wachovia chairman and chief executive officer. "We are deeply saddened by these findings."

6. **Norfolk Southern** railroad also has a history in the slave trade. According to records, The Mobile & Girard company, now part of Norfolk Southern, offered slave

owners $180 each (equals $3,379 today) for slaves they would rent to the railroad for one year. In 1833, Central of Georgia Railway began as the Central Rail Road and Canal Company. Needing to attract investment capital, the railroad changed its name to Central Rail Road and Banking Company of Georgia. The company, aligned with Norfolk Southern, valued its slaves at $31,303, which would equal $663,033 today.

8. **E.W. Scripps and Gannett**-USA Today has found that their own parent company, E.W. Scripps and Gannett, has also had links to the slave trade.

9. According to reports, **FleetBoston** evolved from an earlier financial institution, Providence Bank that was founded by John Brown, a slave trader. Brown not only bought and sold slaves; he owned ships used to transport slaves. FleetBoston financed Brown's slave voyages and profited from them, as a result. Brown, reportedly helped charter the Ivy League school that became Brown University.

10. **CSX** used slave labor to build sections of some U.S. railways. Individual slaves cost up to $200 to rent for a

season – the equivalent of $3,800 today. CSX took full advantage.

11. **The Canadian National Railway Company** is headquartered in Montreal, Quebec. It serves Canada and the mid-western and southern United States. The company also benefited from slavery. The Mobile & Ohio, now part of Canadian National, valued the slaves they lost to the war and emancipation at $199,691. That amount is currently worth $2.2 million.

12. **Brown Brothers Harriman** is the oldest and largest private investment bank and securities firm in the United States, founded in 1818. Former President George H.W. Bush's father and George Bush's grandfather, Prescott Bush, made his fortune on Wall Street as a partner with Brown Brothers Harriman. USA Today found that the New York merchant bank of James and William Brown, currently known as Brown Bros. Harriman owned hundreds of slaves and financed the cotton economy by lending millions to southern planters, merchants and cotton brokers.

13. **Brooks Brothers**, the upscale suit retailer got their start selling clothing for slaves to various slave traders back in the 1800s.

WILLIE LYNCHISM: THE SECRET HISTORY LESSON, A PERSONAL DISCOVERY OF TRUE AMERICAN HISTORY
By Karla "With a K" Edward

15. **AIG** says it has "found documentation indicating" U.S. Life Insurance Company insured slaves. A **U.S. Life** policy written on a Kentucky slave was reprinted in a 1935 article about slave insurance in The American Conservationist magazine. U. S. Life Insurance Company is a subsidiary of **AIG**.

As a student or U. S. Citizen, you may wonder why there is any question about the validity of these accusations regarding major U. S. corporations' participation in the practice of American Slavery. It's because the nature of our country is to sue for financial compensation for damages caused by a perpetrator.

To many, it's called REPARATIONS, a verboten word that may become known as the "R Word" because of its significant meaning for African-Americans. Most people, Black or White, hesitate to talk about what could mean the beginning of what could be a TRUE redistribution of revenue in the U. S.!

According to BBC news, several U. S. corporations, accused of profiting from the slave trade, are being taken to court by African-Americans who are seeking reparations for abuses suffered by their ancestors. These lawsuits are the first of many expected claims against companies like, Aetna, CSX Railroad, Fleet Boston Financial Group and others that profited from the Transatlantic Slave Trade.

As President Barack Obama and other leaders have admonished, we have to be the change we want to see.

Every American must get involved with helping to create the changes that are going to begin to heal the country from its ingrained racism and set it on a path to true morality and integrity in its leadership.

Learning Willie Lynchism: THE Secret History Lesson is a good place to start…

LET'S MAKE A SLAVE

By Willie Lynch

The Origin and Development of a Social Being Called "The Negro"

Let us make a slave. What do we need?

First of all we need a black nigger man, a pregnant nigger woman and her baby nigger boy.

Second, we will use the same basic principle that we use in breaking a horse, combined with some more sustaining factors.

We reduce them from their natural state in nature; whereas nature provides them with the natural capacity to take care of their needs and the needs of their offspring, we break that natural string of independence from them and thereby create a dependency state so that we may be able to get from them useful production for our business and pleasure.

WILLIE LYNCHISM: THE SECRET HISTORY LESSON,
A PERSONAL DISCOVERY OF TRUE AMERICAN HISTORY
By Karla "With a K" Edward

CARDINAL PRINCIPLES FOR MAKING A NEGRO

For fear that our future generations may not understand the principles of breaking both horses and men, we lay down the art.

For, if we are to sustain our basic economy we must break both of the beasts together, the nigger and the horse.

We understand that short range planning in economics results in periodic economic chaos, so that, to avoid turmoil in the economy, it requires us to have breadth and depth in long range comprehensive planning, articulating both skill and sharp perception.

We lay down the following principles for the long range comprehensive economic planning:

1. Both horse and niggers are no good to the economy in the wild or natural state.
2. Both must be broken and tied together for orderly production.
3. For orderly futures, special and particular attention must be paid to the female and the youngest offspring.
4. Both must be crossbred to produce a variety and division of labor.
5. Both must be taught to respond to a peculiar new language.
6. Psychological and physical instruction of containment must be created for both.

We hold the above six cardinals as truths to be self-evident, based upon the following discourse concerning the economics of breaking and tying the horse and the nigger together...all-inclusive of the six principles laid down above.

NOTE: Neither principle alone will suffice for good economics.

All principles must be employed for the orderly good of the nation.

Accordingly, both a wild horse and a wild or natural nigger is dangerous even if captured, for they will have the tendency to seek their customary freedom, and in doing so, might kill you in your sleep.

You cannot rest.

They sleep while you are awake and are awake while you are asleep. They are dangerous near the family house and it requires too much labor to watch them away from the house.

Above all you cannot get them to work in this natural state. Hence, both the horse and the nigger must be broken, that is break them from one form of mental life to another, keep the body and take the mind.

In other words, break the will to resist.

Now the breaking process is the same for the horse and the nigger, only slightly varying in degrees. But as we said before, you must keep your eye focused on the offspring of the horse and the nigger.

A brief discourse in offspring development will shed light on the key to sound economic principles. Pay little attention to the generation of original breaking but concentrate on future generations.

Therefore, if you break the female, she will deliver it up to you. For her normal female protective tendencies will have been lost in the original breaking process.

For example, take the case of the wild stud horse, a female horse and an already infant horse and compare the breaking process with two-captured nigger males in their natural state, a pregnant nigger woman with her infant offspring.

Take the stud horse, break him for limited containment. Completely break the female horse until she becomes very gentle whereas you or anybody can ride her in comfort.

 WILLIE LYNCHISM: THE SECRET HISTORY LESSON, A PERSONAL DISCOVERY OF TRUE AMERICAN HISTORY
By Karla "With a K" Edward

Breed the mare and the stud until you have the desired offspring. Then you can turn the stud to freedom until you need him again.

Train the female horse whereby she will eat out of your hand, and she will train the infant horse to eat out of your hand also.

When it comes to breaking the uncivilized nigger, use the same process, but vary the degree and step up the pressure so as to do a complete reversal of the mind.

Take the meanest and most restless nigger, strip him of his clothes in front of the remaining male niggers, the female, and the nigger infant, tar and feather him, tie each leg to a different horse faced in opposite directions, set him afire and beat both horses to pull him apart in front of the remaining niggers.

The next step is to take a bullwhip and beat both the remaining nigger male to the point of death in front of the female and the infant. Don't kill him. But put the fear of God in him, for he can be useful for future breeding.

Would you favor modifying History lesson content standards, across the country, to include a lesson on "willie lynchism" or Lynch Law?

- Yes   86%
- No, I don't believe it, anyway   9%
- Doesn't matter, it won't change anything.   5%

poll data courtesy of <u>www.karlawithak.net</u>

THE BREAKING PROCESS OF THE AFRICAN WOMAN

Take the female and run a series of test on her to see if she will submit to your desires willingly.

Test her in every way, because she is the most important factor for good economics. If she shows any sign of resistance in submitting completely to your will, do not hesitate to use the bull-whip on her to extract that last bit of bitch out of her.

Take care not to kill her, for in doing so, you spoil good economics. When in complete submission, she will train her offspring in the early years to submit to labor when they become of age.

Understanding is the best thing.

Therefore, we shall go deeper into this area of the subject matter concerning what we have produced here in this breaking of the female nigger.

We have reversed the relationships. In her natural uncivilized state she would have a strong dependency on the uncivilized nigger male, and she would have a limited protective dependency toward her independent male offspring and would raise offspring to be dependent like her.

Nature had provided for this type of balance. We reverse nature by burning and pulling one civilized nigger apart and bull whipping the other to the point of death--all in her presence.

By her being left alone, unprotected, with the male image destroyed, the ordeal caused her to move from her psychological dependent state to a frozen independent state.

 WILLIE LYNCHISM: THE SECRET HISTORY LESSON, A PERSONAL DISCOVERY OF TRUE AMERICAN HISTORY
By Karla "With a K" Edward

In this frozen psychological state of independence she will raise her male and female offspring in reversed roles.

For fear of the young male's life she will psychologically train him to be mentally weak and dependent, but physically strong.

Because she has become psychologically independent she will train her female offspring to be psychologically independent as well.

What have you got?

You've got the nigger woman out front and the nigger man behind and scared.

This is a perfect situation for sound sleep and soundly, for out of frozen fear, his woman stands guard for us.

He cannot get past her early infant slave molding process. He is a good tool, now ready to be tied to the horse at a tender age.

By the time a nigger boy reaches the age sixteen, he is soundly broken in and ready for a long life of sound and efficient work and the reproduction of a unit of good labor force.

Continually, through the breaking of uncivilized savage niggers, by throwing the nigger female savage into a frozen psychological state of independency, by killing the protective image, and by creating a submissive dependent mind of the nigger male slave, we have created an orbiting cycle that turns on its own axis forever, unless a phenomenon occurs and re-shifts the positions of the male and female savages.

We show what we mean by example.

We breed two nigger males with two nigger females. Then we take the nigger males away from them and keep them moving and working.

Say the nigger female bears a nigger female and the other bears a nigger male. Both nigger females, being without influence of the nigger male image, frozen with an independent psychology, will raise their offspring into reverse positions.

The one with the female offspring will teach her to be like herself, independent and negotiable (we negotiate with her, through her, by her, and negotiate her at will).

The one with the nigger male offspring, she being frozen with conscious fear for his life, will raise him to be mentally dependent and weak, but physically strong...in other words, body over mind.

Now, in a few years when these two offspring become fertile for early reproduction, we will mate and breed them and continue the cycle.

That is good, sound, and long range comprehensive planning.

WARNING: POSSIBLE INTERLOPING NEGATIVES

Earlier, we talked about the non-economic good of the horse and the nigger in their wild or natural state; we talked about the principle of breaking and tying them together for orderly production, furthermore, we talked about paying particular attention to the female savage and her offspring for orderly future planning; then more recently we stated that, by reversing the positions of the male and the female savages we had created an orbiting cycle that turns on its axis forever, unless phenomenon occurred, and re-shifted the positions of the male and female savages.

Our experts warned us about the possibility of this phenomenon occurring, for they say that the mind has a strong drive to correct and re-correct itself over a period of time if it can touch some substantial original historical base.

They advise us that the best way to deal with this phenomenon is to shave off the brute's mental history and create a multiplicity of phenomenon or illusions, so that each illusion will twirl in its own orbit, something akin to floating ball in a vacuum.

This creation of "multiplicity of phenomenon" or illusions entails the principles of crossbreeding the nigger and the horse as we stated above, the purpose of which is to create diversified divisions of labor.

The result of which is the severance of the points of original beginnings for each spherical illusion.

Since we feel that the subject matter may get more complicated as we proceed in laying down our economic plan concerning the purpose, reason, and effect of crossbreeding horses and niggers, we shall lay down the following definitional terms for future generations.

1. Orbiting cycle means a thing turning in a given pattern.
2. Axis means upon which or around which a body turns.
3. Phenomenon means something beyond ordinary.
4. Conception inspires awe and wonder.
5. Multiplicity means a great number.
6. Sphere means a globe.
7. Crossbreeding a horse means taking a horse and breeding it with an ass and you get a dumb backward ass, long-headed mule that is not reproductive, nor productive by itself.
8. Crossbreeding niggers means taking so many drops of good white blood and putting them into as many nigger women as possible, varying the drops by the various tones that you want, and then letting them breed with each other until the circle of colors appear as you desire.

WILLIE LYNCHISM: THE SECRET HISTORY LESSON,
A PERSONAL DISCOVERY OF TRUE AMERICAN HISTORY
By Karla "With a K" Edward

What this means is this:

Put the niggers and the horse in the breeding pot, mix some asses and some good white blood and what do you get? You get a multiplicity of colors of ass-backwards, unusual niggers, running, tied to backward-ass, longhand mules, the one productive of itself, the other sterile. (The one constant, the other dying). We keep the nigger constant for we may replace the mule for another tool; both mule and nigger tied to each other, neither knowing where the other came from and neither productive for itself, nor without each other.

CONTROLLED LANGUAGE

Cross-breeding completed, for further severance from their original beginning, we must completely annihilate the mother tongue of both the nigger and the new mule and institute a new language that involves the new life's work of both.

You know, language is a peculiar institution. It leads to the heart of a people.

The more a foreigner knows about the language of another country, to the extent that he knows the body of the language, to that extent, is the country vulnerable to attack or invasion of a foreign culture.

For example, you take a slave, if you teach him all about your language, he will know all your secrets, and he is then no more a slave, for you can't fool him any longer and *having a fool* is one of the basic ingredients of and incidents to the maintenance of the slavery system.

For example, if you told a slave that he must perform in getting out *'our crops'* and he knows the language well, he would know that *'our crops'* didn't mean *'our'* crops, and the slavery system would break down, for he would relate on the basis of what *'our crops'* really meant.

So you have to be careful in setting up the new language for the slave or he would soon be in your house, talking to you as *'man to man'* and that is death to our economic system.

In addition, the definition of words or terms are only a minute part of the process.

Values are created and transported by communication through the body of the language. A total society has many interconnected value systems.

All these values in the society have bridges of language to connect them for orderly working in the society. But for these bridges, these many value systems would sharply clash and cause internal strife or civil war, the degree of the conflict being determined by the magnitude of the issues or relative opposing strength in whatever form.

For example, if you put a slave in a hog pen and train him to live there and incorporate in him to value it as a way of life completely, the biggest problem you would have out of him is that he would worry you about provisions to keep the hog pen clean, or partially clean, or he might not worry you at all.

On the other hand, if you put this same slave in the same hog pen and make a slip and incorporate something in his language whereby he comes to value a house more than he does his hog pen you got a problem. He will soon be in your house.

(Courtesy Black Arcade Liberation Library; 1970 --Recompiled and reedited by Kenneth T. Spann)

When I found this "economic plan" I was astounded. Astounded because it outlined, specifically, the reason Black Americans have so many problems---emotional, economic, social, financial, legal and most importantly, psychological. It was an economic plan that enabled this country to thrive, but caused generations of African Americans to become profoundly dysfunctional.

With this knowledge, I could make personal changes in my thinking, my life and my relationships, but I would be alone in my enlightenment. So many Americans suffer the residual effects of American Slavery and do not even know it! I needed to share this knowledge in an effort to begin the healing process for all Americans, Black, White, Latino, Asian and more!

As a 21st century teacher in the Los Angeles Unified School District, albeit a Substitute, I learned about the emphasis put on "Content Standards" by the behemoth, government mandated, re-authorized, education legislation known as, No Child Left Behind.

Each state has its own "content standards" for each subject matter that is taught in public school. *That* is how I would expose this hidden lesson---get public support to add it to the National History Content Standards.

I started with the online petition. Perhaps this book comprised of the speech, the economic plan, the signatures and the signer's comments will be the impetus that takes this effort to the next level.

I was encouraged to see that so many Americans relate to the need of revising our history textbooks to include "Willie Lynchism." While this is not a popular issue, it is time to take the covers off of it.

Below are signatures and impassioned comments by people who found this petition online without any promotion or advertising.

They must have been looking for an answer to something, in their spirit. I hope they found that part of the answer is to begin their own "self-healing" from the residual effects of American Slavery and Willie Lynchism.

To add your signature to the petition, go to: http://www. PetitionOnline.com/mod_perl/signed.cgi?Wilynch&1

Thank you to everyone who signed this petition. You are an indelible part of this effort as it goes through its process.

'

WILLIE LYNCH LESSON ONLINE PETITION

1.   Karla A. Edward

To: U. S. Congress

I, Karla A. Edward, a citizen of the United States, former broadcaster and educator in the Los Angeles Unified School District, hereby petition the U. S. Government to modify the National History Content Standards to include a comprehensive lesson about the Willie Lynch Speech of 1712 and the subsequent "Lynch Law," which defines the origin and development of the social being called the "Negro."

I believe that this hidden lesson of our nation's history needs to be taught to our children and acknowledged by adults who missed it, so the root cause of racism in America can truly be understood.

Only through acknowledgement of "Lynch Law," confession of its wrongdoing and the forgiveness of those who have been "willie lynched," can Americans, Black and White, begin to heal from our past and look forward to a healthy psychological future of true peace, justice and inclusion.

Sincerely,

All Who Have Signed

SOURCE: http://www.PetitionOnline.com/mod_perl/signed.cgi?Wilynch&1

SIGNERS AND COMMENTS

In Favor Of Adding Lesson To The
NATIONAL CONTENT STANDARDS FOR HISTORY

SOURCE: http://www.PetitionOnline.com/mod_perl/signed.cgi?Wilynch&1

Signer #	Name	Comments
1.	**Karla E**	
2.	**Nakema J**	
3.	**Gloria B**	
4.	**NICHOLE**	

5. **TENISIA M**

6. **Melissa D**

7. **Paris R**

8. **Tamika J**

9. **Arleezah M**

10. **Stan G**

11. **WYNISAH**

12. **Harve C**

13. **Angela C**

14. **Anna M**
    We have no future if the truths of our past are not revealed to us and to our children. Thank you so much for realizing the importance and the relevance of these letters.

 WILLIE LYNCHISM: THE SECRET HISTORY LESSON, A PERSONAL DISCOVERY OF TRUE AMERICAN HISTORY
By Karla "With a K" Edward

15. **Robert H**

16. **Tony**

17. **Donald F**

18. **Joseph Daniels I**

19. **Ulysses T**

20. **Patricia H**

21. **David White I**

    Let's shed the shackles of our past and start to build anew.

22. **Kabrina D**

    I am currently working in a public school system as a high school teacher, and I have always wondered why did some of my black students display signs of hatred for each other, why they display signs of a nonchalant attitude for education, and why they just simply act the way that they do. After reading the Willie Lynch Speech,

I now have a better understanding. Yes, I totally agree that this speech should be put in history books as a lesson to be learned. But until that is done, we as educators, community leaders, and parents can do all that we can to educate our black brothers and black sisters about this lesson.

23. **John A E**

24. **Kendrick Jr.**

    I sign and agree with this petition.

25. **Ray**

26. **Rheta S**

27. **Dianna**

28. **WILLIAM B**

    The Law of Quantum Acoustics, expressed through MC3=E3

29. **Theresa**

30. **James H S**

31. **Leonard T**

32. **Tamara A C**

33. **Ralph Worley S**

34. **Kristal**

> I also feel outraged that this very important and historical document was not taught to me in all my years of education. Until my Senior year in High School, I was ignorant to who Willie Lynch was and what role this {dead} man holds in my life or ancestry. The only reason why I was taught this information was because a Muslim teacher in my High School created and wrote up his own curriculum outline to a class he knew that his people needed to be educated about, which was African American Literature. I feel just as Carter G. Woodson felt: " Our students are taught to admire the Hebrew, the Teuton and to despise the African'" in The Mis-Education

of the Negro. I was not taught, in depth, about the Triangular slave trade, or the many other factors I SHOULD have been enlightened and knowledgeable about while growing up in a land in which I was not wanted at one point and, in some hearts and minds, still not wanted.

35. **Maurice J**

36. **Cheryl S**

After reading the letter I wanted to cry. I'm 49 years old and I wish I read that when I was a child/young lady. Every Black Woman bearing children needs to read about W.L. in order to start changing the cycle. It all starts at the beginning and we have to change the way we raise our black males. KNOWLEDGE IS POWER.

37. **Krystal P**

I feel that as a black American woman, I am entitled to know all of my history about who I am. I think not only should I have to know, but also all Americans need

WILLIE LYNCHISM: THE SECRET HISTORY LESSON, A PERSONAL DISCOVERY OF TRUE AMERICAN HISTORY
By Karla "With a K" Edward

to know our history. We have to learn ALL of European American history, why not ALL of African American history.

38. **Chivonne H**

39. **Ahmad A**
    The contents of The Petition are short however it says a lot and yes it is about time.

40. **Tynisha H**

41. **Tara Ross P**
    I've never heard anything about the Lynch Law until it was spoken about on a movie.

42. **Abraham J**
    The implications are profound, and definitely should be taught in schools if we, as a country, are serious and sincere about combating racism in America. This becomes especially necessary as an educational mechanism and can be an important tool, since the Willie Lynch

matter shows, at the very least, the intimate and initial roots of racism and its birthplace in 1712, on the banks of the St. James River, Virginia.

43. **Nakiya N J**

This is a vital part of our history & needs to be taught to our children! I'm 20 years old & am just learning the origins & history of it & am ashamed that I didn't already know about willie lynch & I wish that I would have been taught it in school!

44. **Dominic M**

45. **LAKIESHA CARMAINE A**

46. **Dianna Simmons H**

Stop Lynching NOW…

47. **Kevin Y**

48. **Kenneth J W**

To know where we must go is to know where we have been and what has influenced our destiny here in the United Sates.

49. **Gail S**

50. **Gregory G H**

51. **Tascha S**

52. **Christina J R**

53. **LaTonya**

54. **WESLEY F**

55. **Eric K. Greene I**

56. **Karla A E**

57. **Kimberle E**

58. **Schevon T**

59. **Thomas M**

60.   **Patrice B**

I stumbled upon the Willie Lynch speech browsing on an African American website. several years ago and I'm studying his part in history for my History 240 class.

61.   **Shannon B**

62.   **Valerie N G**

63.   **Nicole P**

64.   **Linda J**

Give us Our Freedom; why are we fighting?

65.   **Ba'ylon C**

66.   **Robert L Wilson I**

67.   **Nathan H**

68.   **Jabbaar E**

69.   **Camille C**

WILLIE LYNCHISM: THE SECRET HISTORY LESSON,
A PERSONAL DISCOVERY OF TRUE AMERICAN HISTORY
By Karla "With a K" Edward

70. **Tiffany P**

71. **Torri B**

72. **Tyler C**

73. **Gail G**

74. **Aidan Y**
    This is important. Talking about racism in the classroom and otherwise is a necessity for our country's future and well-being.

75. **Abena J A**

76. **Andre D G**

77. **Brian A**

78. **Arsenio W**

79. **Audrey Lee J**
    I agree.

80. **Lee E. W**
   The Time is Now.

81. **Gibran G**

82. **Chantea W**
   Teach the complete history. Offer African American history course options to all high schools help prevent history from repeating itself.

83. **Cherice R**
   We will be repaired if there is a God.

84. **Christopher A**

85. **Ray C**

86. **Elizabeth H H**

87. **Derrick I**
   It's very important to know, as Americans trying to understand the effects of American slavery.

88.   **Mitchell R**

I agree that the whole of America has been Willie Lynched, with Black America receiving the brunt of that lynching, which is still at work in this country today. I believe that it does need to be addressed, taught to all Americans so that we can all understand the race and class terrorism that it promotes...and then dismantle it.

89.   **Alfonse B**

This speech is the fabric of what America is built on.

90.   **Eric**

91.   **Darius R**

I think we should've all got this long ago. The only history we got was being bought and sold like objects.

92.   **James C**

It's about time.

93. **Elizabeth G**

I believe like you do, that willie lynch's lesson should be taught to everyone so we can understand why whites hate blacks and why they think that they are better than we blacks. No one race is better than the other; we are all filthy rags in the eyes of God.

94. **Dave R**

Stay strong.

95. **Eliza J**

The former Secretary of Education, William Bennett said recently (Sep 05) that the crime rate would go down if every Black child were aborted. Wouldn't the crime rate go down if every Black child were educated? Where is this self-proclaimed virtuous man's heart? His thinking is a crime. It isn't just Blacks that need this knowledge. Clearly, all Americans would benefit. The psychological and institutionalized hatred and greed is sinful.

WILLIE LYNCHISM: THE SECRET HISTORY LESSON, A PERSONAL DISCOVERY OF TRUE AMERICAN HISTORY
By Karla "With a K" Edward

96. **Kevin J**

I agree and will support this effort fervently.

97. **Erica McCowan, B**

It is time to teach true history not lies!

98. **Latiff B**

99. **Joanne B**

100. **John J**

101. **Kenneth S H**

102. **Charles B**

We need to make this change immediately.

103. **Joyce W**

104. **Mrs. Jennifer D. H.**

105. **JEANETTE**

In fact, all our history books in public school should be required to be accurate and represent the actual historical occurrences not just what makes white America look good. That would include the truth about the Native American Indians and the role Congress had in the systematic genocide of Native American Tribes.

106. **Danielle M**

We need to heal or acknowledge the past to build a healthy future. All they have for us is prison and poverty. Our behaviors that have come as far back as slavery, but is slavery really far back, when we exhibit the behaviors of our ancestors hurt and struggle?

107. **SHAVON T**

AFTER READING THE WILLIE LYNCH LETTER I BECAME FRIGHTEN BY THE REALITY OF THE LETTER. IT MADE ME FEAR FOR OUR CHILDREN'S FUTURE STATE OF MIND, AS WELL AS MY OWN, AND HOW I DEAL WITH MY SURROUNDINGS. I BELIEVE THAT IN ORDER TO REMEMBER

LIFE LESSONS YOU MUST REVIEW IT FROM TIME TO TIME. I THINK THIS WOULD BE A STEPPING STONE IN HISTORY.

108. **Kamal Islam M**

We need to know our past, so it will not be repeated.

109. **Linda S**

I totally agree. There is a lot of black history missing from the U.S. educational system.

110. **Tiffany T**

If this is true, we need to get this out so that we can move forward to a better future.

111. **Ira T**

This needs to be shown. Understanding history will make America stronger, because of differences.

112. **Lannis M**

I had tears in my eyes as I read and realized that we were conditioned to act a certain way...and it worked.

113. **Kema F**

I believe they need to be made aware of why we behave the way we do towards each other.

114. **Kendal S**

Good stuff!

115. **Kelly S**

I greatly appreciate your efforts however, I hope that you don't think that reparations is the answer. I think that we need to use this letter to show our problems to ourselves (Americans) and then after some time we can move forward to reparations. Also I think that we need to make those that are calling themselves biracial classify themselves as such. Because at this rate, in 20 years, I think the black population will be down

WILLIE LYNCHISM: THE SECRET HISTORY LESSON, A PERSONAL DISCOVERY OF TRUE AMERICAN HISTORY
By Karla "With a K" Edward

from 13% to 9%! REALLY. What will our reparations count for if only given to a bunch of non-black people. Seems that the more time goes on the lighter we are getting in this country. And ironically the more we are accepted. Don't believe me look at some old pictures of the civil rights movement.

116.   **Tenisha M**

This hidden history is an important part of my life as well as the lives of others, and I feel this should be taught to all children to help understand that they don't have to live a life full of all these negativities expressed through this speech. But can change history for our people and show that not all people have to feed into these illiterate concepts set out for our people to fail in this economy.

117.   **Adrian S**

They should have taught it when I was in school.

118. **Naquan N. B**

119. **Miltonia R**
     This is Very important !!!!!!!!!!!!!!!!!

120. **Neal K**

121. **Michelle L. J**
     This is a much-needed lesson so that our young people can understand how the slave mentality still permeates through our community. They have not been taught their history and must know that their behavior plays into the Willie Lynch Methodology.

122. **Nicholas L. W**

123. **Patreece Y**
     Willie Lynch's letter needs to be taught in every public school in the United States.

124. **Nicole W**
     It is an integral part of history that needs to be recognized abroad.

125. **Monique Sherrie Kelley B**

We must know where we have been to know where we are going.

126. **Clarence F**

127. **Aseelah G**

128. **Yaminah M**

I fully agree that this should be taught in school.

129. **Nancy N**

We need our children to know about this NOW, more than ever!!

130. **Petra T**

131. **Sharmaine N**

I am very sad that most African Americans do not know about Willie Lynch. It should be mandatory that this Letter is learned in school. I strongly believe it would change the thoughts of African Americans.

132. **Michael W**

Any means necessary.

133. **Ruth B**

134. **RYAN W**

Lets tell the REAL truth to our students.

135. **Maritza F**

136. **Shirley A C**

It's about time...everyone should know how it ALL started!!!

137. **Keasha**

Interesting.

138. **S.T. D**

The missing piece of THE BLACK HERITAGE PUZZLE.

139. **Tienna L**

This is so very important, to the sociological growth of an African American.

WILLIE LYNCHISM: THE SECRET HISTORY LESSON, A PERSONAL DISCOVERY OF TRUE AMERICAN HISTORY
By Karla "With a K" Edward

140. **Tracy W**

141. **Clayton N**

142. **Robert C**

143. **Stephanie M**

It is about time that we recognize our so-called "founding fathers" for who they really were.

144. **Deborah E**

145. **Rena J**

Please enter this information in the history classes. This is very vital information for our community as a whole. I know that this can make a major difference in a positive way when it is taught right. This is a start in the right direction for those who really have the heart and courage to do what's right. Thanks for allowing me to give my expression.

146. **J M**

147. **Nita Y**

Please free the rest of the world especially this country.

148. **Veronica C**

149. **Robert Cotton**

150. **Tarvis C. G**

Knowledge is power and everything in this life is a mind-set. In order for us to be free we must first change our minds sets and believe God has allowed this to happen for a reason. God knew what he had created when he created the "African American Race". He knew we would be the better for it. He knew that if we could handle the process we would surely be able to handle the blessing. So now we must empower each other to become educate on the cycle that had our minds confused.

WILLIE LYNCHISM: THE SECRET HISTORY LESSON,
A PERSONAL DISCOVERY OF TRUE AMERICAN HISTORY
By Karla "With a K" Edward

AFTERWORD

According to www.factcheck.com, Robert Lopresti, a librarian at Western Washington University, found in his research that twelve U. S. presidents owned slaves and eight of them were slaveowners while a sitting president.

The last president to own slaves was, ironically, Ulysses S. Grant, who was elected President in 1868 after he and Union forces won the Civil War. Grant owned a slave named William Jones, whom he freed in 1859.

Futurist Magazine contributor, Joseph F. Coates wrote in the May-June 2003, issue an article called, "Updating the Ten Commandments." In rewriting commandment #3, he writes, "Recognize our societal and genetic histories and work to mend their flaws. Rather than passively deplore the flaws in our social history, such as slavery, we should strive to fix whatever negative repercussions still linger."

By his thoughtful statement with future generations in mind, Mr. Coates probably supports the goal of the Willie Lynchism petition and this book.

Do you believe you've been "willie lynched?"

- Yes, I guess I have.   74%
- No, that is in the past. It didn't touch me.   11%
- Hell, NO!   15%

poll data courtesy of www.karlawithak.net

This is a question for you to answer for yourself today.

Now that you are fully aware of this evil, insidious, political, economic, social, financial hate crime that enslaved Africans, to benefit wealthy Caucasians/Europeans, what will you do, in your world, to overcome the manifestations of, what I call, "willie lynchism?" Are YOU living a "willie lynched" life?

WILLIE LYNCHISM: THE SECRET HISTORY LESSON,
A PERSONAL DISCOVERY OF TRUE AMERICAN HISTORY
By Karla "With a K" Edward